Tattling

Joy Berry

Illustrated by Bartholomew

Joy Berry Books
New York

This book is about Tami and her brother, T.J.

Reading about Tami and T. J. can help you understand and deal with tattling.

You are tattling when you report someone else's wrongdoing.

When you tattle on someone, you can hurt the person's feelings or get the person into trouble.

There are many reasons why you might tattle. You might tattle because you want attention.

You might think that tattling will get someone to notice you. But tattling will not get you the kind of attention you want or need.

Thus, you should not tattle to get attention.

You might tattle to make yourself seem better than others. You might want to make others appear to be bad so that you will appear to be good.

But tattling can make you seem bad instead of good.

Thus, you should not tattle to make yourself seem better than others.

You might tattle because you are too lazy to solve your own problems. You might want others to solve your problems for you.

But you should solve your own problems if you can.

Thus, you should not tattle so that someone will solve your problems.

You might tattle because you want to hurt other people's feelings. You might want to get other people into trouble.

But you should never do anything to hurt others.

Thus, you should not tattle to hurt other people's feelings or get them into trouble.

Tattling might bother the people you tattle to.

They might become annoyed.

They might become angry with you.

Tattling will most likely upset the person you tattle on.

The person might become angry with you.

The person might not want to be around you.

Tattling can be harmful to others and to yourself.

But this does not mean you should never tattle.

You must report a wrongdoing if a person's life is in danger.

You must report a wrongdoing if a person's property is in danger.

Ask youself this question before you tattle: "Am I going to tattle because I want to help someone or because I want to hurt someone?"

Tattle only if you are doing it to help someone.

Ask yourself another question before you tattle: "Have I done all I can to help solve the problem?"

Do not report a wrongdoing unless you have done all you can to help solve the problem.

Sometimes you might see someone doing something wrong.

Think of how you would want to be treated if you were that person.

Help the other person do what is right if help is needed.

Try not to tattle unless someone's life or property is in danger.

It is important to treat other people the way you want to be treated.

If you do not want people to tattle on you, you must not tattle on them unless it is necessary to do so.

Joy Berry Enterprises
146 West 29th St., Suite 11RW
New York, NY 10001

Cover Design & Art Direction: John Bellaud
Cover Illustration & Art Production: Geoff Glisson

Production Location: HX Printing, Guangzhou, China
Date of Production: February 2010
Cohort: Batch 1

Printed in China
ISBN 978-1-60577-136-6